I0605403

If You Would Let Me

Also by Maggie Dietz

Perennial Fall

That Kind of Happy

If You Would Let Me

Maggie Dietz

Four Way Books
Tribeca

for you

Library of Congress Cataloging-in-Publication Data

Names: Dietz, Maggie author
Title: If you would let me / Maggie Dietz.
Other titles: If you would let me (Compilation)
Description: New York : Four Way Books, 2026.
Identifiers: LCCN 2025027277 (print) | LCCN 2025027278 (ebook) | ISBN 9781961897809 trade paperback | ISBN 9781961897816 ebook
Subjects: LCGFT: Poetry
Classification: LCC PS3604.I375 I4 2026 (print) | LCC PS3604.I375 (ebook) | DDC 811/.6--dc23/eng/20250625
LC record available at https://lccn.loc.gov/2025027277
LC ebook record available at https://lccn.loc.gov/2025027278

This book is manufactured in the United States of America and printed on acid-free paper.

Four Way Books is a not-for-profit literary press. We are grateful for the assistance we receive from individual donors, public arts agencies, and private foundations including the New York State Council on the Arts, a state agency.

We are a proud member of the Community of Literary Magazines and Presses.

Contents

“But what the gods give, we humans endure, painful as it is, for our necks are under the yoke.”

—Homeric Hymns

If You Would Let Me

If you would let me hold you I could breathe
Your purple hair, the flakes of makeup breaking
From your boiling eyes. You'd see how much you need

Cool words. Outside the door I've heard you seethe
Through years of trouble. I'd press away the shaking
If you would let me hold you. I could breathe

The atoms of your dreams, my face so close I'd eat
Your anguish, taste the tang of black tears leaking
From your locked-down eyes. You'd see how much you need

To forgive, to be forgiven, to reach and cleave
To something incorruptible and unforsaken.
If you would let me hold you I could breathe

Away your brinks, lay cushions underneath
Your cliffs. I'd let no shiv of light be taken
From your arctic eyes, you'd see. How much you need!

Is there no salve, no balm in Gilead
To breach the brick and thistle of your hatred?
If you would let me hold you I could breathe.
Your broken eyes would see how much you need me.

∞

Don't Go

Autumn reminds us with numb precision
It isn't safe to love.

Its arias of attrition intone
Our fated anguish.

You reap sings the pungent
Field *what you sow.*

I swear I was just snipping daffodils, surprising
You with a jar of them on your desk!

Remember that? And when you said you
Loved me more than the green of summer?

Ironies abound. The absconding songbirds
Chitter about chickens coming home.

The morning glories double down,
Trumpeting purple across the trellis.

Why must my grief
Be the gate

You leave through, frozen
Ajar on its ancient hinges?

Nobody

You needed a hand
a help a harbor
needed a rind
of bread a pat
on the back a pallet
a skillet a coat
in a snowstorm You craved
entertainment
blueberries salmon
itched for an antidote
a bridge over rapids
an iodine pill
in a meltdown some
fennel and salt

You wanted time
and air and silence
a nap and a shower
a new duvet You
asked for a pillar
a dollar some cover
and nobody answered
nobody showed You called
for an ambulance airlift

a medic for anyone
someone to blame and
explain you but no one
did anything nobody
heard your face

Middle School

Persephone and her friends brought
Waxed paper cups of ice cream
To the meadow by the river.

They tasted each other's flavors.
Their laughter made ripples a heron
Mistook for alewives underwater.

Under some of their shirts,
The first hiccups of puffy nipples.
They huffed webbed dandelions whose

Wishes floated in the air with a pop song
Throbbing tinnily from a neon phone.
Ants gathered on a plastic spoon.

Who knew the earth would open?

It was Tuesday in a small town.
They lay on their backs daydreaming
Into each other's pierced ears.

Metamorphosis

Because I liked to bring the outside in
I had on my desk a painted bowl with
Three stones in it like eggs in a nest.

I liked to brood over them, to thumb
Their surfaces and think.

They were so gentle, a kind of pure
Potential. One afternoon

I cropped up monstrous, ghost
Of all you couldn't control.

Looking for anything to lob, you lifted
The largest as I stood across the room.

Later I iced my collarbone and restored
The barren stones to the world.

Persephone's Friends

When her story tore open, they ghosted.

Dandelion gossamer, ducklings paddling
Hell for leather into the cover of cattails.

Then they biked into the blue afternoon
Of average adolescence. At home

They sulked in clothes-strewn bedrooms
And griped about setting the table.

They unfollowed her on Instagram
And blocked her cell. They cropped her

Out of images and didn't say her name
Except to agree she never really was

That great a friend and maybe she was
Asking for it braless in that tank top.

Metamorphosis

Sometimes you seemed to want to make
Something dazzling from your rage.

You knew I liked it: the antique mirror
I'd bought at a dusty storefront run by sisters.

You grunted when you swung it from
The wall and flung it to the floor.

For an instant bits of slivered
Glass fell up like inverted rain.

Sure enough, it cut me.

And it took years to pull
The crumbs of glass out of the wool.

Infancy

When we were alone on that peak,
Just the two of us breathing

The impossible air together
Like a tired chimera,

In a gas of heady love and hormones
I swore I'd keep you safe forever

And we believed me, fools
That that place made us

*

O privacy of hinged bodies, of hunger
And defecation

Simplicity of the washing machine's
Low gurgle,

Soft static on the monitor—

O relics of a vanished
Impregnable past

Montauk Daisy

Now's no time for
brightness, the kids'
breath at the bus
stop blooming clouds,
but that smug bush
will serve its sunny-
side-up doilies
well into October.

The fall my father
died I cut it back—
its vernal grass and
citrus scent tasteless
to a mouth of dust.

It only grew back
bigger. All fall it
cannot stop its vulgar
pantomime of spring.

A killing frost
the only cure.

Evening Snow

December and wine-dark leaves still cling
To the dwarf maple in the yard.

Dusk imparts its radiant arrangements:
Slivers of time affixed in gaps between branches,
Mosaic tiles or bits of painted glass.

The jigsaw scene is all together now.
The brown shed silvers in the twilight.
Red leaves hunch on splintered limbs:

Last year's leaves obscured by altered water,
Ancient weather, like the dull old dual
Aches of memory and desire. The snow

A lilac amnesia, blown through
The latticework of the world.

Glacial

For weeks the kettle steamed
Its aching siren, singing deep
Into this house of ice.

Now even the lamp of my longing
Is spent, a jumble of
Moths in the globe.

Nothing outside survives, but
Errant spores have breathed black
Peonies onto the shattered plaster.

From the empty bed
Upstairs the springs uncoil
A warped refrain: *You made*
This cold, now live in it.

Am I even awake?
Are those embers or icicles
Cracking in the grate?

Cerberus

One mouth eats the hand that feeds it.
One tongue soothes and binds a wound.
One mouth oozes its forever hunger

Into a moonless river. One nose scents
The trails of specters, one flares toward
Every fleck of meat, one lifts only

When the icy air unfurls ambrosia.
One throat growls fire, another
Thirst. One jowl revs, another wilts.

One jaw commands a phalanx of
Fangs, and one surrenders its catch.
Two ears are pricked for whips

And two for hooves. One furred
Muzzle drips limbs from its hinges,
One has never seen a seed of blood.

One nape cranes toward a caress,
One chokes against its ruff of chains,
One swans into uneasy sleep.

One mind is ever somewhere else,
One flushes pheasants in its dreams,
One rages in its cave of bone.

One body bears it all.

Lament

Before you were born I gave
You the meadow I gave you
The soil the seed and the plough
I gave you a home in my body
A home in my house in my temple
The reverence of people my thin
Tapered ankles I made you immortal

I made you a mirror of everything
Precious I made you a basin of nectar
Ambrosia a bed of narcissus shot
Through with stars later I let you
Unravel and tantrum I let you
Coat your eyes with ash and dye
Your hair a thunderous sunrise

I let you I gave you I held
You I made you but I couldn't
Save you I couldn't save you

Emergency Fugue

if this is a true life the little dog laughed
hang up and the clinician will as a shepherdess
should in thirty to sixty days diddle diddle
return your ring around the rosy and call it
macaroni if this is a life what is your reason
to speak to the hickory dickory doctor he's
here we go round the press zero to speak to
he's going to the fair he's here we go he's eating
christmas pie! sing he sing ho sing hang up
the phone the kittens have gone to saint paul's
hang up and dial and how many times has
the little lamb sat on a wall? nine ten a good
fat hen! 9-1-1 what's your hot cross buns?
a man of words and not of deeds is not a thread
and needle though all the words he ever spoke
were fiddle faddle feedle! are there any
fol de riddle firearms in the house? lol de riddle
no sir and are there any pills? . . . hush-a-bye
baby go over the stile go to the stable the night
is so raw it's raining it's pouring cock robin
farewell the wind is in the east and pussy's in
the well a branch gave way and simon fell . . .
and hickory dickory who'll toll the bell?

Lily of the Valley

Under the erased
elms of my childhood
I first heard the
tongueless bells
sirening their white
tune into April.

I didn't yet
have the word
enchantment
but that is what it was
to sit among them
in the shade.

They touched
a part of me I
hadn't met.

My mother told me
they were bad and not
to touch. There was a
baby in a bassinet.

Without a word,
I fell in love with
paradox: poisonous
baby bonnets,
lethal lace.

Childhood

One day in the woods I was suddenly scared of the slender birches,
their thousand
bovine eyes, the way they would corporealize among the coarser
trees, bright wicks
lit with trembling yellow tears. Up close they held out scrolls to
decipher.

When desolation chooses you there is at first the feeling of being a
little flattered.

Another day I hollowed out a snowbank to shelter a scrap of
newspaper, an ink-mottled
page from a Red Owl sale flyer I believed to be alive because the
wind kept beating it
up against my heels as I walked home from Queen of Angels
Elementary where in
Sister Mary Fran's room baby mice and chipmunks floated in Ball
jars of formaldehyde.
I wanted everything to have a soul.

Even then I lived for springtime, for the slice of light angling
between the window frame
and vinyl shade. It is human nature to mistake relief for love.

I could never predict anything. And I thought when there was
    nothing left to imagine
I would be relieved. I tried to imagine it.

Metamorphosis

Now and now and never often
Enough or bright or light or dark
Enough this need to change the filter
Find the right who in the mirror
With the right hair

The trip to Walgreens always an
Emergency: something semipermanent
To stave off changes scored in stone

Your roots are ravaged, stunned
By bleach so the hair hardly grows
Now and short shed bits get wet
And stain the countertop with
Stubborn threads of red and
Blue and black and red again

In the sunlight—which you keep
From your dark room with ice blue
Strip lights streaking like a scar
Along the ceiling—I have seen

A halo of prismatic fire flaring
From the tips of your split ends

Mummy

Over plates of quinoa and mango chicken it appeared
out of a closet, resurrected from a dusty hatbox
and passed around like a sleeping infant:
a three-thousand-year-old sixteen-year-old girl.
Or parts of a girl: the forearms and head, the body
maybe taken for its rags to make brown butcher paper.

The hatbox had bloomed from a larger box
labeled by a child's hand with black magic
marker GREEK ARTIFACTS, brimming with other broken,
ancient things—cracked kylix, one-horned terra-cotta bull—
and stowed next to a box coughing tinsel, marked XMAS,
and another marked WEDDING GIFTS, evidently
lugged unopened house to house since the long-ago wedding
of our just-divorced host.

Inherited Victorian plunder, curiosities bought up by
one of George Washington's descendants whose legal woes
our friend's grandfather fixed, he said, pouring more Pinot.

Football season, and one guest yelled "Go long,"
faked lobbing the head across the room.
Another pretended to use an arm as a back scratcher.
Everybody laughed. I laughed.

I took the head in my hands.
Just above the temple, a hole so you could see
the yellow skull, the wrapping parted like hair.

I passed the head and took an arm.
Where the wrap had frayed at the tips
of the fingers were brown fingernails, the wrists
slashed where looters had snagged a bracelet,
a hole below the knuckle of one finger.

Then from the same box our friend produced
a broken falcon: walnut head, the severed body
narrowing like a bottle-stopper, the wings dried
tobacco leaves closing over its breast.

Horus, son of Isis, sun-god, sky-god, god of protection:
Had they killed the bird to bury her with it?

Somebody's beloved child, long-dead
daughter of the long-dead:

Days were when she watched the bird circle
and dive and later pinched mites from its feathers
with her fingernails, her rings catching sun, scattering

seeds of light. Late afternoons, she'd laugh and hitch up
her gold and pomegranate robes to run, teasing the boy
who'd given her the bracelet—carnelian and feldspar—
until he caught her small bright body in his arms.
She kissed him. His breath warmed her neck.

Metamorphosis

Because the face you saw was not the one
You wanted you made with a bright steel brad

Two cockeyed holes in the skin between
Your brows and bled all over the barbell

You tried to ram through them half
Laughing in the TikTok I saw later at the way

The silver stud ends skewed diagonal.
You told me that the marks were acne scars

But fessed up the day you used a safety pin
To stab the weblike membrane connecting upper gum

To lip and asked if you could keep it as if
The mutilation were a kitten or a frog.

What was I supposed to say? That I like
Your face the way it came?

I did what any brokedown woman would and drove
You to a place called *Pierced Utopia* at

The Saugus mall where a human with a spangled face
Plunged a needle through your perfect nose.

Stargazers

It hurts how
much they want
to be alive:

Blush vulvas
sprung from snug
green pods grenading
into spangled showgirls
to declare summer
half over.

Jayne Mansfields
of the garden bed,
they outpink even
the potted fuchsia.

It makes no sense
their stems don't
need a stake.

I can hardly suffer
their coquettish
carpe diem bosoms
bobbing in the sun.

Would that I could crush
the sealed buds open—
to get the scab
without the cut.

Metamorphosis

The bluish underside of your left arm is
From wrist to elbow latticed with white
And pink lines. The madness of their
Overlapping is like a game of pick-up sticks.

The stakes are graver, the lines a ladder
Leading to the next time you need
To try to get the hell out of you.

The little windows between the lines
Recall the times we'd draw with
Sidewalk chalk teetering hopscotches
The length of the whole block and
Throw pea gravel from under the gutters
To show us how far we could go on
The Sisyphean path to starting over again:

Never long enough to make
The game go on forever.

Adolescence

My mother used to say if I was late *I pictured you dead in a ditch* so then I had to
picture myself dead in a ditch, face-down in stagnant water next to a seeping culvert,
leaves in my sodden hair. Sometimes there was a snapping turtle nibbling at my ear
and purple chicory and invasive Dame's Rocket bowed over my back like a casket spray
under a dirge of crickets and wind and a waxy moon. *Be careful what you wish for* I said
once to my mother so I could watch the water brim in her blue eyes.

To Gertrude Ophelia appeared *incapable of her own distress.* An old-person way
of seeing things. Ophelia, sick of everybody's shit, shuffled off this mortal coil in
a swirl of bawdy songs and wildflowers. Two men who'd variously used her grappled
in her open grave trying to outgrieve each other. Her death was beautiful and effective.

There were some nights I sang my corpse to sleep: *good night, sweet lady, there's*
a daisy, there's rue for you. She was only mine, and dear to me.

Trembling Hills

Then I wake up in the ward.
No doctors, no patients. Alone at last
In the white quiet. Nor am I

A patient but a presence like
A jellyfish or hummingbird or
Lattice of a leaf. I'm almost

Not there. No shatterproof
Mirrors, no mirrors at all. Nothing is
As it was, the rooms empty

Of bolted-down beds;
Walnut-lacquered floorboards,
All the doors thrown open in

The labyrinth of corridors.
I know the only way
To the garden is through

An attic window. When I
Pull the recessed ladder I
Whiff dust smoldering on years

Of forgotten boxes. I'm
Climbing now. I'm almost
There. I'm practically floating.

I can almost see the searing
Green and hear the leaves and
Bees' wings, almost breathe

The bright of spruce and juniper,
Almost reach the cool rills of water
Thrilling over the fountain tiers.

Privacy

My grandmother pulled cheer infinitely out of herself like a train
of knotted scarves. Babies, too, seemed to unfurl endlessly until
the ninth one almost killed her. Quiet was scarce. She implored the plaster
and the chandelier *please help me Jesus give me strength* so frequently
the toddlers thought God lived in the ceiling. *I can't have a moment's*
peace she huffed, face crumpling at the altar of the ironing board, when
the elder daughters, my aunt and mother, padded down at night
assuming she'd enjoy their company.

A mother contemplates her kids never existing only in the alcove
of her mind where the thoughts are safe from God.

When I knew her, she spoke breezily about the stucco days: abundant
bunnies in backyard cages, soap and spray starch and road trips where the
little ones hunched on upturned buckets on the floorboards of the Oldsmobile.

Never having existed is not the same as ceasing to exist:
A mother cannot let even a crack of light onto that cross.

She brought me from a trip to Moscow with my grandfather a set of
Matryoshka dolls
and I imagined the biggest to be the mom of all five babies sprung
from
her severed middle. My grandmother's doll would have been big as
a bowling pin: in the hallway, framed Christmas pictures of the
kids lined up like a blonde staircase in front of the fireplace.

All of Nana's children lived and all of them outlived her.
I never used to see it for the miracle it is.

There was another picture, of her, at seventeen: lipstick that even
in black and white is red, a sequined dress licking heeled dance
shoes,
her hand arced into the air, dark hair coiffed into a cloud,
cheekbones angling for the stars.

Leave No Trace

No gate, no main entrance, no ticket, no ranger. Not far
From where Frost once raised chickens and ill-fated children, near
Where the Old Man's glacier-hewn face though bolstered to
Its godlike roost by rods and turnbuckles slid
From our fledgling millennium into oblivion,
You can cross the Pemigewasset on a bridge
Then, compass-north but southbound on the trail,
Ascend an old grassed-over logging road
To the carved-out collarbone of Cannon Mountain.

This is Lonesome Lake. How you go from here
Depends on why you've come: to out a spruce grouse
Or listen for the *whee-ah* of a Bicknell's thrush;
For a breezy picnic or a midlife crisis,
A long haul or a day trip to some cascade.

Bring for your purposes only what you need:
Salmon jerky, a canteen or CamelBak,
Band-Aids, a ratchet and strap, a roughed-up heart.
Bring sunblock, a notebook, the Beatles, Beyoncé,
The Bhagavad Gita, a Bible, some Hitchens or Hegel.

However long you stay you must leave nothing.
No matchbox, no pole-tip, no grommet, no cup.

Carry in and out your Clif Bar wrappers,
Your fear of bears and storms. Keep the rage
You thought you'd push through your boot soles into the stones,
The grief you hoped to shed. If you think you've changed,
Take all your changes with you.
                                                    If you lift
An arrowhead from the leaves, return it. Pocket
No pinecone, no pebble or faery root. Resist
The painted trillium even if its purple throat
Begs to be pressed between your trail guide's pages.

∞

The Things I Do

Before I burned the earth I tore my hair someone
could have stopped me then the branches I ignited
were to seed my search a speeding bird I scoured
land and sea for my lost cause my stolen seed and no
one said a fucking word to me the silence fed my
silence fed my grief I went inside myself I didn't
wash or eat I hid inside a hood and cropped up
old under the olive trees

                                        Before I burned the earth
I loved another woman's baby someone could have
stopped me let me raise him let me love him like
I hid him from his mother in a cleansing fire a
metal brand I claimed him tried to save him from
his mortal fate he wasn't hurt the opposite his
useless mother wrenched him back that bitch
I turned another boy into a newt in tears his
mother watched me do it call me savage why
should someone else have what I can't

                                                        After that
there was no stopping me I quit my job I held a
razor to Earth's wrist my own I bent the tools broke
the plows I hid the seeds and choked the field with

stubborn grasses scourged the yield with rot I called
the shots I cut the shoots I summoned rain and sun
and hungry birds I let small children starve and cows
with calves I am not proud but what choice did I have
like corn and barley they were mine to kill and I would
have what's mine by any means you stupid humans
still can't seem to gather can't begin to glean
it was for love I burned the goddamned world

Someone Else

I entered someone else's suffering and when I
Surfaced I looked behind me into the sheen of it.

We'd been to the bottom, the muck of scales and femurs
Of trees. I'd communed with the dead, my dead, to make

Sense of the sunless depths. They rocked me—father,
Grandmother, friend—in arms of slippery weeds that moved

Like flames. Later the pond was a river that writhed,
A worm at the end of a line on a map I couldn't follow.

So many burps and lurches, so much pull. After I was
Dry I saw my old hopes were ants in the bathroom,

My life's work an absurd pageant, that I had been
Alone and stupid, trying to steer the current like a mule.

There had been no we, no sense, no fire underwater.
In the mirror of the river a silver river inched like a fish

Along a woman's scalp. I was supposed to know
This woman. I was supposed to love her.

High School

When Persephone walked in the laughing
Stopped. A childhood friend spoke louder,
Pretended not to hear her, when she asked
If she could sit. She took her ham sandwich
And hunched with her pants and knees
Up in a dented stall. She wasn't hungry.

*

Persephone tried out various disguises.
In town the boys on bikes would bark
At her. Cars slowed down to holler *trick*
Or treat or flip the bird, *hey freak*. The blueberry
Muffin stayed inside its case; the library
Book on its shelf; the kid in her bed.

*

You're not the only kid here has it hard,
The teacher said when Persephone wouldn't
Lift her head. You're smart but lack initiative.
After Persephone's pencil had filled a page
With eyes, she raised her hand for help. How dare
You tell me how to do my job, the teacher said.

*

All day the kids at school talked up the party.
Now the pictures pinged onto her phone—
French maid in fishnets vaping Os, zombie grinding
With a cat, the kid too cool to wear a costume.
Persephone sat on the steps, a plastic cauldron
Of candy on her lap, waiting for angels and ghosts.

Hermes

The deeper I got in the fathoms of darkness
The more lost I was from even the idea of light.

In the airless room I found Demeter's daughter
Slack as a cadaver, the girl she was almost
Invisible: wax cheekbones cupping chasmal wells.

Lifting her off the sofa was like trying to hold
A dream in your head at the edge of sleep.

Hell was cold so I buttoned my coat.
I pressed a stethoscope to her temple and heard a quiet,
Unkempt scuffling like a mouse behind a wall.

I asked to borrow the chariot that swept
Her up those months ago.

That's how it is: the way out of
Hell looks a lot like the way in.

On Lithium, Vraylar, Lamictal! I called
To Hell's immortal horses.

Metamorphosis

I wanted you to want to go. I texted
Photos of the rutted mountains,
A firepit next to a spring-fed lake,
A rented house of hand-hewn logs
Somebody's grandpa built decades ago.
You sent back a rolling-eye emoji.

Not your idea of a good time, even when
All the eyes on you had made you want
To zip yourself forever into the bed-tent
You dragged me to buy. Whatever.

But you were drawn to the muslin water
Unperturbed by motors. There was no dock.
To swim you had to scrabble down
Broad slabs of metamorphic rock.

You'd stay in for hours, even after we'd
All dried and drifted off. Not as cold
As the Atlantic, you said. Fewer sharks.
Of course we'd have to go back home where
The phone would hawk its fake refrains
Into your face, but for days the only echo,
Staccato and sharp as an arrow, was a mother
Grebe teaching her young to fish.

When you were alone I watched you from
The window, just for safety, sorry, watched
The water buoy your body and close around
Your face and knees as you bobbed honest
As a log and feet from you a pelican floated
Its prehistoric body into the sky.

So I saw you erupt from the rocky bottom
Into the air like the rockets we used to
Light off in the yard, the water flaring from
Your hair and suit like molten ore and you
Were far away but you were smiling.

Reprieve

High summer after the lilacs and it feels
Like the days never end. The morning
Glory seedlings have just begun to nose
Their way onto the poles, furred vines
Sentient as snails. The dog luxuriates
Sideways in a rectangle of sun, only
Moving to nip the air when a bumblebee
Trundles by, furbished in gold.

Flightless chicks open their throats,
All hope. The sedum is only green
And green. The apples, too, and hard
As marbles. Everything is only about
To happen and you are here turning
Cartwheels in the grass as I turn the pages
Of a book I don't intend to finish.

Come sit with me and I will be your shade
Tree as we rock on the glider through
The long afternoon, adrift on the river
Of the cicadas' endless, spectral tune.

False Indigo

These blue mouths
eating light at
the creek side,
I could kiss them.

Like the smell
of opals or the
sound of stones
the weightless
blue moths
flock onto the
branches.

They too can make
exquisite dye: blue
the way brass is
bright, the way
jazz is fast.

Daring and
improbable as
love, their color's
true the whole blue
month of June.

Trick Narcissus

She'd wandered away from her lazing friends
To watch a cormorant scissor its wings
In the sunlight and there among the bull thistle
And foxtail—names her mother taught her—
Was a hundred-headed cluster of ruffled jack snipes
Ablaze like a bouquet of fallen stars.

The snapshot she posted did nothing
To capture the scale, the smell, the crenellated
Madness of the swooping blooms.

When she tugged the stem it was as if she
Swung the lever of a roller coaster and out
From the earth boiled a blur of hooves. She
Roared for her parents until she couldn't breathe,
Until the soil closed over her like the sea.

On some stray thread there must exist the day
Persephone picks the prize narcissus and brings
It home. Demeter loves how the fracas of petals
Fireworks against the off-white wall! The fruit
Of a single bulb brims over a big enamel bucket,
Sweetly stinking up the house until they toss it
On the compost heap and get on with their lives.

Metamorphosis

In white sunlight we unzipped the lid
Of the habitat, a miniature pop-up hamper.

The butterflies had arrived by mail,
Still worms, spindled and sharp-looking,

Little tailless seahorses, unfurling in
A plastic tub with goo at the bottom

Like suet—the caterpillars' food, dotted
With frass. I didn't point out that they shit

Where they eat or that Painted Ladies
Sounds like a polite term for prostitutes.

We were to keep them misted and away
From bright windows. The webbing

Wasn't worrisome, we read—in the wild
It kept them stuck to plants and they could

Pull the silk to close a leaf around them
And hide from bad guys. For days nothing

Happened. You hunched next to the buffet
Watching yourself watch them in the mirror.

From the doorway I watched the way
Your hair curled at the base of your neck

As you sweated, the way your T-shirt when you
Sprayed the mister showed your tan lines.

You were there when one let go a ghost,
A gauze of skin almost too soft to see.

After we moved the paper disc affixed
With shivering chrysalides, after more

Boring thrilling days of waiting, the pods
Darkened and the first one ruptured

Into a crumpled butterfly, a balled batik
Handkerchief spilling from a pocket.

Next came the slow calico explosion,
The beating and pulsing that burst

The wings into being. You may not
Remember but I do: you were beside

Yourself, pulsing, triumphant. Four
Hatchings and two days of sugar water

Later it was time to let them go. You weren't
Sad—we'd read it was the right thing.

You toted the mesh cylinder out to the
Picnic table and opened the flap just enough

To let one land. A leftover scuff of polish
On your fingernail. Your teeth still short

And rounded, two rows of sugar-pearl corn.
The sun shone down as one by one

You gave them to the sky.

Missing Song

A violin shut in a case shelters
Notes no bow may ever find.

The close-mouthed crocus
Shouts its color into a dark core.

Sound found my skin, the sea of blood
Where silver fishes mounted

An orchestral frenzy spelling
Danger. I knew, I knew

When seeds of ice pebbled my neck
And blistered into a hundred little suns.

In my body's branches the bluebirds blackened
Then scattered into embered ash,

Making flares of the trees, my brain
A fog of bees so thick I couldn't see,

Oh, but I knew, I heard. The kindred
Don't need ears:

The deer in my heart thundered
Into the thicket and disappeared.

Did you hear, then, the tears that dripped
Around your wrist into a crystal bracelet?

Did the little socks and mittens of my singing
Keep you warm?

You must know what I mean even if
You do not know you know: Child,

When you called my name I heard you
Though your cries could find no wind.

Embrace

Years I think I spent in the kitchen wishing
The imprint of your herringbone sweater into
My skin. Years disrobing potatoes, pinching
Salt, hoisting scalding cast iron onto racks.
My ear on your shoulder, fug of oysters
And strawberries from under your lifted arms.
Months on months of spelt and thyme and
Crisped chicken thighs. My back a door
Your hand thumped softly. Years I folded
Napkins into birds, set plates you'd transfer
To a tray and take upstairs. I moved the
Chairs to mop but you'd outgrown the game
That made the hallway row of them a train.
When I made the eggless cake nobody
Laughed when vinegar hit the hump of soda.
Your coarser hair, a cruder color, mopped
My cheek. Whole calendars elapsed with
Me kneading and whisking and you
Notching inches onto the wall. Years I was
The vinegar. Moon upon moon, cans
In and out of the pantry. You didn't even
Clear your throat the afternoon you found me
Hunched at the cutting board, back to the
Door, wearing my stained striped apron.

Cusp

Thank god it's March, thank god it's raining,

The water gnawing the last crusts of snow
In the yard where a lone crocus parts its lips.

Just days now until a chorus of color
Will welcome you back, the cold

Ground greening to meet you and
Pansies blinking up from the mulch.

*

Yesterday I woke to find the branches
Tipped with green and purple flames.

Earlier each day now the window frames
The dawn. I see your face in every square

Of the calendar the sun pins to the floor.
I'm baking bread with flour from last year's wheat.

I washed your favorite sheets and filled
Your room with hothouse tulips.

*

I know you'll come, but when?

A late frost mocks the sparks
Of my insatiable impatience.

*

Soon enough the irises will don
Their ballgowns underneath the elm.

Soon enough the hyacinths
Will quiver clustered bells.

Inevitable angel, hasten home.

*

Spring after spring after spring
The frogs outsmart the underworld.

Evenings on the screened-in porch
I hold my breath and listen for their song.

Instead of Epigraphs

"Nobody"

"No one, either of the deathless gods or mortal men, heard her voice."
—Homeric Hymns, tr. Hugh G. Eveyln-White

"Man disavows, and Deity disowns me."
—William Cowper

"Glacial"

"But, now, uncertain of the length
Of this, that is between,
It goads me, like the Goblin Bee –
That will not state – its sting."
—Emily Dickinson

"Emergency Fugue"

"You parents all that children have,
And you, too, that have none,
If you would have them safe abroad,
Pray keep them safe at home."
—Nursery Rhyme, trad.

"Childhood"

"This thing of darkness I / Acknowledge mine."
—William Shakespeare (Prospero in *The Tempest*)

"The Things I Do"

> "...Behold, / how the world looks, minding / your mother."
> —Louise Glück, "The Pomegranate"

> "Ceres and Earth discharge a common function: the one lends to the corn its vital force, the other lends it room."
> —Ovid *Fasti* I, tr. G.P. Goold and James G. Frazer

"Hermes"

> "Demeter's daughter, her whom none may name, by secret schemings Plouton, men say, stole, and then he dropped into earth's depths, whose light is darkness."
> —Diodorus Sicilus, tr. C. H. Oldfather (Sicilus quoting the poet Karkinos)

> "Grief and terror were still to be seen in her features, / yet she was nonetheless queen of that shadowy kingdom."
> —Ovid, *Metamorphoses,* tr. Charles Martin

"Reprieve"

> "How delightful is the breeze:—so very sweet; and there is a sound in the air shrill and summerlike which makes answer to the chorus of the cicadae."
> —Socrates, in Plato's *Phaedrus,* tr. Benjamin Jowett

"Metamorphosis" ("I wanted you to want to go")

> "...the / patina of circumstance can but enrich what was / there to begin / with..."
> —Marianne Moore, "Black Earth"

"Trick Narcissus"

"From its root a hundred heads grew out and a perfumed odor; the whole broad sky and the whole earth smiled, and the salty swell of the sea."

—Homeric Hymns, tr. Martin L. West

"Missing Song"

"...and the heights of the mountains and the depths of the sea ran with her immortal voice: and her queenly mother heard her."

—Homeric Hymns, tr. Evelyn-White

"Embrace"

"He brought them to a halt where fair-garlanded Demeter was waiting, in front of her fragrant temple, and when she saw them she rushed forward like a maenad on the shady-forested mountain."

—Homeric Hymns, tr. West

"Trick Narcissus"

> "From its root a hundred heads grew out and a perfumed odor; the whole broad sky and the whole earth smiled, and the salty swell of the sea."
> —Homeric Hymns, tr. Martin L. West

"Missing Song"

> "...and the heights of the mountains and the depths of the sea ran with her immortal voice: and her queenly mother heard her."
> —Homeric Hymns, tr. Evelyn-White

"Embrace"

> "He brought them to a halt where fair-garlanded Demeter was waiting, in front of her fragrant temple, and when she saw them she rushed forward like a maenad on the shady-forested mountain."
> —Homeric Hymns, tr. West

Acknowledgments

Grateful acknowledgment is made to the editors of the publications in which poems in this book first appeared, some as earlier versions: *The Adroit Journal*; *AGNI*; *Bennington Review*; *Birmingham Poetry Review*; *Literary Matters*; *On the Seawall*; *Plant-Human Quarterly*; *Ploughshares*; *Plume*; *Salmagundi*; and *Tar River Poetry*.

"If You Would Let Me" appeared also in *2023 Pushcart Prize XLVII: Best of the Small Presses.*

"Leave No Trace" was commissioned by the Academy of American Poets for the Imagine Our Parks with Poems series.

Thank you to Ryan Murphy, Martha Rhodes, and everyone at Four Way Books.

Thank you to UMass Lowell and Jentel Arts for gifts of time and community.

I have some friends without whom I don't know who I am: Robert Pinsky is the North Star; Louise Jarvis Flynn never fails to center me; Sandra Lim is the best work wife anyone could ask for; Jill McDonough knows all the stories and reads all the poems; Kelly Alexander, Ashley Carson, and Julie Cevallos: thank you. Emily Meehan, Genny Moriarty, Eimer Page, and Molly Simmons: thank you.

My mom deserves a huge shout-out for her sturdy, steadfast support. To my siblings Brian Dietz, Kristin Dugan, and Colleen Dietz: thank you.

Todd Hearon, you hold the center, and my heart.

Lionel and Kipp, you have taught me so much. You are the perfect kids for me.

About the Author

Maggie Dietz was born and raised in Green Bay, Wisconsin, and educated at Northwestern University and Boston University. She is author of the poetry collections *That Kind of Happy* and *Perennial Fall*, which won New Hampshire's Jane Kenyon Award. Dietz was the founding director of the Favorite Poem Project, created by former U.S. poet laureate Robert Pinsky, and is co-editor of three anthologies related to the project. Her awards include a Pushcart Prize and fellowships from the Fine Arts Work Center in Provincetown, Phillips Exeter Academy, the New Hampshire State Council on the Arts, and Jentel Arts in Wyoming. Her work has appeared in *AGNI, The Adroit Journal, Bennington Review, Birmingham Poetry Review, Ploughshares, Poetry, Salmagundi, The Threepenny Review* and elsewhere. She teaches at the University of Massachusetts Lowell and lives in New Hampshire with her family.

Four Way Books is grateful to those individuals who participated in our Build a Book Program. They are:

Anonymous (10), Robert Abrams, Debra Allbery, Maggie Anderson, Kathy Aponick, Sally Ball, Jean Ball, Victor Basta, Adria Bernardi, Richard Blanchard, Laurel Blossom, adam b. bohannon, Lee Briccetti, Anthony Cappo, Anne Babson Carter, Cyrus Cassells, Jennifer Christman, Peter Coyote, Kwame Dawes, Michael Anna de Armas, Brian Komei Dempster, Patrick Donnelly, Lynn Emanuel, Joan Frank, Rigoberto González, Rachel Eliza Griffiths, Catherine Grossman, Naomi Guttman and Jonathan Mead, Beth Harrison, Jeffrey Harrison, KT Herr, Carlie Hoffman, Melissa Hotchkiss, Thomas and Autumn Howard, Parker Howe Foundation, Catherine Hoyser, Linda Susan Jackson, Elizabeth Jackson, Liz Janik, Marilyn Johnson, Deborah and Maria Jonas-Walsh, Elizabeth J. Kandall, Maeve Kinkead, Lindsay and John Landes, David Lee and Jamila Trindle, Rodney Terich Leonard, Howard Levy, Owen Lewis and Susan Ennis, Ralph and Mary Ann Lowen, Maja Lukic, Ricardo Alberto Maldonado, Donna Masini, Cleopatra Mathis, Lupe Mendez, Dale Neal, Mary Jane Nealon, Kathy Nelson, Marilyn Nelson, Nicole Nevadunsky, Kimberly Nunes, Rebecca and Daniel Okrent, Cathy McArthur Palermo, Marcia Pelletiere, Megan Pinto, Martha Rhodes, Paula Rhodes, Laurie Rosenblatt, Lyris Schonholz, Soraya Shalforoosh, Jennifer Skeele, Mary Slechta, Page Hill Starzinger, Sarah Stone, Yerra Sugarman, Marjorie and Lew Tesser, Reed Turchi, Maria Walsh, Martha Webster and Robert Fuentes, Calvin Wei, George Whalen Jr., Mark Wunderlich, Kathleen Zimmerman, and Carol Zoref.